Ancient Egyptian Jobs

John Malam

D0550843

Heinemann
LIBRARY

Milne's High School

06975

www.heinemann.co.uk/library
Visit our website to find out more information about **Heinemann Library** books.

To order:
☎ Phone 44 (0) 1865 888066
📄 Send a fax to 44 (0) 1865 314091
💻 Visit the Heinemann Bookshop at www.heinemann.co.uk/library to browse our catalogue and order online.

First published in Great Britain by Heinemann Library, Halley Court, Jordan Hill, Oxford OX2 8EJ, part of Harcourt Education Ltd. Heinemann is a registered trademark of Harcourt Education Ltd.

© Harcourt Education Ltd 2002
First published in paperback in 2003
The moral right of the proprietor has been asserted.

All rights reserved. No part of this publication may be reproduced, stored in a retrieval system, or transmitted in any form or by any means, electronic, mechanical, photocopying, recording, or otherwise, without either the prior written permission of the publishers or a licence permitting restricted copying in the United Kingdom issued by the Copyright Licensing Agency Ltd, 90 Tottenham Court Road, London W1T 4LP (www.cla.co.uk).

Editorial: Nick Hunter and Jennifer Tubbs
Design: Jo Hinton-Malivoire and Tinstar Design (www.tinstar.co.uk)
Illustrations: Art Construction and Geoff Ward
Picture Research: Maria Joannou and Virginia Stroud-Lewis
Production: Viv Hichens

Originated by Ambassador Litho Ltd
Printed in China by Wing King Tong

ISBN 0 431 14583 0 (hardback)
06 05 04 03 02
10 9 8 7 6 5 4 3 2 1

ISBN 0 431 14588 1 (paperback)
07 06 05 04 03
10 9 8 7 6 5 4 3 2 1

British Library Cataloguing in Publication Data
Malam, John, 1951 –

Ancient Egyptian Jobs – (People in the Past)
331.7'00932

Acknowledgements
The publishers would like to thank the following for permission to reproduce photographs:
AKG London pp. **4**, **26**, **38**; Ancient Art and Architecture Collection pp. **8**, **11**, **12**, **21**, **24**, **29**, **40**; Ancient Egypt Picture Library pp. **28**, **34**, **41**; The British museum pp. **20**, **27**; Philip Cooke/Magnet Harlequin p. **13**; Peter Evans pp. **6**, **36**; Manchester Museum p. **43**; Photo Archive/J Liepe p. **22**; Wellcome Trust p.**14**; Werner Forman Archive pp. **10**, **16**, **18**, **30**, **32**; Dr Caroline Wilkinson, Unit of Art in Medicine, University of Manchester p.**42**.

Cover photograph of fishermen on a boat reproduced with permission of the Ashmolean Museum.

The publishers would like to thank Dr Christina Riggs for her assistance in the preparation of this book.

Every effort has been made to contact copyright holders of any material reproduced in this book. Any omissions will be rectified in subsequent printings if notice is given to the publishers.

20295904

MORAY COUNCIL
LIBRARIES &
INFORMATION SERVICES
J331.700932

Contents

Words appearing in the text in bold, **like this**, are explained in the Glossary.

Egypt – the gift of the Nile

The mighty River Nile winds its way through the deserts of North Africa. Thousands of years ago the great civilization of ancient Egypt grew on the river's banks. This book tells the story of the people who worked to make ancient Egypt great, from the priests of Egyptian temples, to the workers who built the monuments that have survived to this day.

Egypt's mighty river

The civilization of ancient Egypt would have developed very differently if it had not been for the River Nile. The Nile provided the people of Egypt with water for drinking, bathing and watering their crops. Its fish and birds were caught for food. It was also the country's most important highway, used by boats to transport people, animals and goods. Even more importantly, the River Nile was the source of ancient Egypt's rich fertile soil. The ancient Egyptians lived and worked along the fertile strip of land watered by the Nile's annual flood. It was the only area where they could grow crops. Beyond it lay the vast, sandy desert. Few people lived there, and food could not be grown because it was too dry.

A land of workers

There are many ways to find out about the ancient Egyptians. This book looks at some of the many different kinds of work they did and how it contributed to ancient Egypt's society. No matter how humble or ordinary that work was, it served a purpose and was important.

The River Nile is the world's longest river. From its source in Burundi, East Africa, to where it empties into the Mediterranean Sea, it measures 6670 kilometres (4145 miles) long. The people of ancient Egypt lived close to the river, on its floodplain, which was a narrow strip of fertile land.

On a map you can see how the sites of ancient Egypt lie close to the River Nile, spaced out along it. It was easier to travel by river than on land. Boats floated downstream (south to north) on the river's current, and when they sailed upstream (north to south) they were helped by the prevailing wind that blew in from the Mediterranean Sea.

It is worth remembering that it is people that make a society what it is. The people of ancient Egypt created a strong society that lasted for around 3000 years. No other society, ancient or modern, has lasted this long. For example, our own modern industrial society is only around 300 years old – ten times shorter than the timeline of ancient Egypt!

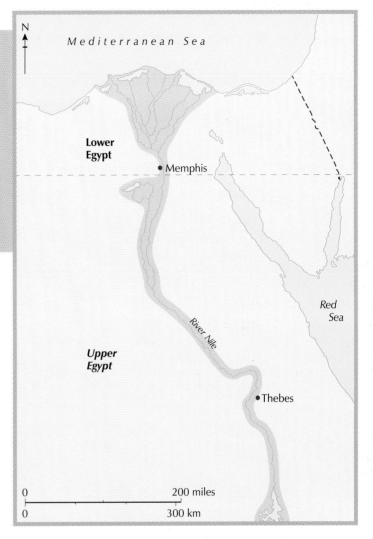

Three thousand years of history

The beginning of ancient Egyptian history is usually dated to about 3000 BC. There are several reasons why this date is used: it was when Egypt became one land, when the separate kingdoms of Upper and Lower Egypt were united to make one country and the first pharaoh (king) ruled the country. It was also when the first specially built tombs were made, and the first **hieroglyphs** (signs) were used for writing. Of course, much happened in Egypt before 3000 BC, but it was from this date onwards that the civilization of ancient Egypt began to flourish. For the next 3000 years pharaohs ruled Egypt until, in 30 BC, the last of them died, and Egypt became part of the Roman world.

Who worked in ancient Egypt?

We can find out about the workers of ancient Egypt from the remains that have survived from the time and from what was written down by the Egyptians or visitors to Egypt. The problem for people studying the past is knowing what to believe.

Herodotus and the story of the slaves

When the ancient Greek historian Herodotus visited ancient Egypt, he asked people about the country and its past. He wanted to learn about the history of Egypt, its customs and its buildings. He was very interested in the famous Great Pyramid at Giza. Herodotus was in Egypt around the year 450 BC, which was some 2000 years after the massive pyramid had been built.

Herodotus probably asked questions such as: how old is this pyramid? why was it built? how was it built? Don't forget Herodotus was a foreign visitor, a man who had travelled to Egypt from faraway Greece. What's more, he was asking questions about events that had happened centuries before his own time.

The pyramids at Giza. This famous group of pyramids was built by the pharaohs Khufu, Khafre and Menkaure. Khufu's pyramid was the first built, and is known as the Great Pyramid. The pyramid built by Khafre, Khufu's son, (in the centre) only appears larger because it stands on higher ground. At the top of Khafre's pyramid traces of its limestone outer casing still survive.

Perhaps the people Herodotus spoke to did not know the answers to his questions – the old pyramid had become as much a puzzle to the Egyptians as it was to Herodotus. Or perhaps people were keen to impress the stranger in their midst, to show-off, so they made things up and Herodotus believed them. He used the information he gathered to write a book. When he wrote about the Great Pyramid, built for the pharaoh Khufu, Herodotus said:

- the pharaoh forced his people to work for him – they were slaves
- 100,000 slaves worked constantly
- it took twenty years for the slaves to build the Great Pyramid.

The making of myth

Did Herodotus get it right? Was the Great Pyramid really built by slaves? Until recently people believed that slave labour was a vital part of ancient Egyptian society. They believed this because Herodotus, whom historians call the 'father of history', usually got his facts right. However, others have called him the 'father of lies', because some of his so-called facts have been proved to be wrong.

Today, we know that the story told by Herodotus, about how the Great Pyramid was built by slaves, is just that: a made-up story. There *were* slaves in ancient Egypt, but not on the scale described by Herodotus.

The slaves that never were

Recent work by **archaeologists**, on a site close to the Great Pyramid, has revealed a 'pyramid city', where workers and officials lived with their families. It seems that most of the workforce only stayed a short time at the building site before returning to their homes throughout Egypt. New gangs of workers then took over from them. Modern archaeology has changed the way we think about workers in ancient Egypt. Out goes the old idea of mass slavery, invented by Herodotus, and in comes the idea of a willing and well-organized workforce.

Organizing the workforce

It has been calculated that the population of ancient Egypt was never more than around 5 million people. Organizing the people was the key to Egypt's success – and one of the reasons why the civilization lasted for so long.

One kingdom, one pharaoh

Before the arrival of the first pharaoh, Egypt was not one country, but two. In the north was the kingdom of Lower Egypt, which was closest to the sea. In the south was the kingdom of Upper Egypt, which was higher up the course of the River Nile. Each kingdom had its own rulers, until a king from the south conquered the land in the north. The identity of this king is something of a mystery, but he is usually identified as King Narmer. He became Egypt's first pharaoh, in about 3000 BC. Narmer's conquest of Lower Egypt brought the two kingdoms together. Egypt became one country with its capital at Memphis, 25 kilometres (15 miles) south of Cairo, the modern capital of Egypt.

Most ordinary people in ancient Egypt worked on the land, growing crops and tending to farm animals. However, they could be called upon at any time to work on a project for the state. If this happened they had to obey instructions given to them by officials. Because ancient Egypt had this system of compulsory labour, major projects, such as the building of a pyramid, were possible.

From pharaoh to peasant

Narmer was the first in a long line of pharaohs. Altogether we know of around 170 of them. These all-powerful men, and sometimes women, ruled Egypt for 3000 years, until the last of them died in 30 BC. During all this time, the pharaoh was Egypt's most important person. People thought of him or her as a god on Earth – a god-king. The pharaoh was Egypt's head of state, in charge of the government, the economy, the law and the army. Like all leaders, he had many people to help him. It was these officials who were responsible for the day-to-day running of Egypt.

The most important official was the **vizier**, who was like a modern-day prime minister. There were some times in Egypt's history when there were two viziers, one for Upper and one for Lower Egypt. The vizier was called the 'chief of all the king's works'. His job was to carry out the orders and decisions of the pharaoh. He was in charge of tax collection and public works. He was also in charge of governors called **nomarchs**. The nomarchs were the officials who controlled Egypt's many districts, or **nomes**. Ancient Egypt was divided into 42 nomes, each with its own mini-capital, towns and villages.

Beneath the nomarchs were the **scribes** and **overseers** of each district. Scribes were record-keepers and overseers supervised the peasants. It was the peasants who formed most of Egypt's population, and it was these ordinary people who were the nation's workers.

Slaves in ancient Egypt

There were few slaves in ancient Egypt before the time known as the Middle Kingdom (about 1938 BC to 1600 BC). From then on foreign prisoners captured in Egypt's wars with her neighbours did become slaves. They were forced to work on building projects, and on the land where they ploughed fields and ground grain to make flour for bread. Egyptians, too, could become slaves. These were people who had fallen into debt, or who were too poor to feed themselves. The only way out of their troubles was to sell themselves into slavery. This way they could settle their debts, in return for food and shelter.

The scribe

Most people who lived in ancient Egypt could not read or write. The few people who did learn reading and writing were mostly men: women rarely learned these skills. Men who mastered reading and writing were privileged members of society, and they belonged to a special class of workers known as **scribes**. Women could not become scribes so they did not need to read and write.

A scribe's education

At the beginning of Egyptian history, in the time known as the Old Kingdom (about 2575 BC to 2130 BC), scribes passed on their knowledge from father to son, in their own homes. This system was eventually changed to one in which boys were sent to special schools. The schools were built within the grounds of temples, to which they were linked. They were called 'Houses of Life'.

Boys went to school from the age of four or five, whereas girls did not go to school at all. Boys learned to write by copying out words and passages from well-known texts over and over again. They wrote their school exercises on many different materials, such as pieces of broken pottery and flakes of limestone, or on wooden boards that could be wiped clean and then re-used. By the time he was sixteen years old a boy was ready to leave school, and start work as a professional scribe.

To write, a scribe sat cross-legged on the ground. He pulled his **kilt** or skirt tight against his knees, which made a flat surface for him to rest on. He wrote with a reed brush or pen, held in his right hand. He used his left hand to hold and unroll the papyrus roll on which he wrote. A scribe named Khety said, 'It's the most important of all occupations. If you can write, you will be better off than everyone else.'

The work of a record-keeper

Scribes were record-keepers, and in Egypt's highly organized society it was important to have detailed, written information. They recorded just about everything – from brief notes about how many cattle a farmer owned, to long reports for the **vizier** about the progress of work on the pharaoh's building sites. Scribes also copied out religious, scientific and historical texts. They drew up contracts for the sale of land and goods, and wrote and read letters for ordinary people who could not do it for themselves.

Paper to write on

A scribe's most important writing material was **papyrus**. It was a kind of fine white paper, made from the pith (the soft inner part of a plant stem) of the papyrus water reed. Reeds were gathered from the banks of the River Nile, their tough outer stems were removed, and the pith was cut into thin strips. Two layers of pith strips were placed together at right angles, then beaten until the plant fibres became a single flat sheet, about 50 by 40 centimetres. Sheets were joined together to make rolls. There were usually twenty sheets in each roll, but rolls themselves could be joined together. The longest known papyrus roll is more than 40 metres in length.

When scribes wrote, they usually used an everyday script that was quick and easy to use. At first they used a script called **hieratic**. Hieratic was used for hundreds of years, until it went out of fashion around 600 BC. From then on scribes preferred an even simpler script, called **demotic**. As well as being able to write and read these two scripts, scribes could also use Egypt's most famous script – **hieroglyphs**. To write Egyptian hieroglyphs, scribes had to learn more than 700 different signs. Hieroglyphs were slow to write, and their main use was for writing **sacred** texts.

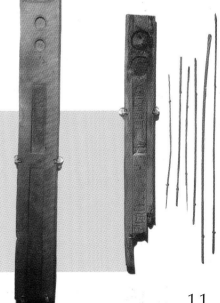

A scribe carried his brushes and pens in a wooden writing case. Most writing cases had two hollowed-out circles, where the scribe mixed his writing inks. He made black ink from soot or charcoal, and red ink from a **mineral** called ochre. Water was added until the ink was the right consistency with which to write. The ink took time to dry, and the scribe was careful not to smudge his work.

'Servants of the gods'

Every Egyptian believed the same things about how the world had been created, and how it was governed by the same major gods. People's religious beliefs were passed down from one generation to the next, which was how it had been for as long as anyone could remember.

Priests worked in Egypt's temples. The Egyptians believed that their gods actually lived inside the temples, that these were their homes on Earth. It was the duty of priests to serve Egypt's gods by offering them gifts and prayers, and to be in charge of religious ceremonies and rituals. Because of their devotion and loyalty to the gods, Egyptian priests called themselves 'servants of the gods'.

Entering the priesthood

Both men and women could enter the priesthood. Women who became priestesses worked as musicians and dancers. Male priests conducted ceremonies, wrote **sacred** texts and helped with the running of the temple's daily business. A person who wished to enter the priesthood had to be 'pure', to show respect for the god whose temple they were to work in. This was the only 'qualification' they needed for the job. Priests were trained in the temple's school, or 'House of Life'.

Priests wore different clothes from other people. This was not only to show they were priests, but it was also another way of showing their purity and cleanliness when they were in the presence of the god they served. A priest's main clothes were made from clean, white **linen**, and on their feet they wore white sandals (ordinary people went barefoot).

Egyptian temples

Temples were far more than places where prayers could be said, and where ceremonies were performed. They were often massive structures. In some towns, several temples were built close to each other, creating sprawling complexes of buildings where hundreds of people worked. There were workshops where craft-workers made objects for use in the temple, **granaries** where grain was stored, schools for **scribes** and priests and libraries where book-scrolls were kept. Temples owned land and mines that made them rich, and because of this they played a major part in Egypt's economy.

Before they could enter the most sacred parts of the temple – the parts ordinary people were not allowed into – priests purified themselves. They chewed **natron** (a type of **mineral** collected from the edges of lakes) and breathed sweet-smelling incense fumes. They washed and cut their finger and toe nails. Male priests also shaved off all their body hair, including their eyebrows. This careful preparation was designed to cleanse their bodies of anything that might offend the temple's god.

Priests and priestesses came from ordinary families. After they had served in the temple for a period of time, they were free to return to their homes to carry on their normal lives.

A temple was a series of rooms, or halls, linked by a corridor. As priests walked along the corridor they felt they were travelling along a sacred route, passing through 'forests' of stone columns. At the end of the corridor was the temple's inner sanctuary. It was a small, dark room that only the most senior priests could enter. Inside was a statue of the temple's god, within which the god was believed to live. Every day, priests washed the statue, dressed it in clean clothes and left food to nourish the god.

The doctor

The ancient Egyptians knew a great deal about medicine, and how to treat injury and illness. As a result, their doctors were highly valued people. When the ancient Greek historian Herodotus wrote an eyewitness account of ancient Egypt in the 400s BC, he said: 'There are plenty of doctors everywhere. Some are eye-doctors, some deal with the head, others with the teeth or the belly and some with hidden **maladies**.' Herodotus was saying that Egyptian doctors specialized in different branches of medicine, just as doctors and surgeons do today. For example, a man called Iry was doctor to one of Egypt's pharaohs. Iry was described as 'doctor to the king's belly', and also as 'the king's eye-doctor'.

Studying to be a doctor

Doctors were almost always men. Just as **scribes** and priests were trained at 'Houses of Life', so too were ancient Egypt's doctors. It used to be thought they gained their knowledge about the human body by helping in the preparation of **mummies**. This would have given doctors the chance to study the body in great detail – inside and out. However, this was probably not the case, and most experts now think doctors had nothing to do with the **embalming** process. Instead, they learned about the human body by other means.

Doctors studied written medical texts. This tablet is inscribed with ancient Egyptian surgical instruments. It forms part of the wall of the temple of Kom Ombo, which was built during the reign of the Ptolemies.

They learned their work by studying medical scrolls and tablets. These were 'textbooks' that contained detailed information about the human body, and how to care for it when it became ill. The information written on scientific scrolls represented a vast amount of medical knowledge, which had been learned by the Egyptians over the course of hundreds of years.

Treating the sick and injured

Like today's doctors, the doctors of ancient Egypt were trained to talk to and observe their patients before they treated them. They asked them how they felt, how they had injured themselves and so on. They did this to learn about a patient's **symptoms**. Only when they had recognized the symptoms did doctors make a **diagnosis** and offer a treatment. They were trained to recognize and treat around 200 types of sickness.

Healing by magic

If the usual forms of medicine failed to cure a patient, doctors turned to the powers of magic. Some of the prescriptions they offered must have been really horrible, especially ones that involved the use of blood, urine and even animal faeces! They can only have been intended to drive out evil spirits that were held responsible for a patient's troubles. Some patients preferred to sleep in special rooms inside temples, where they hoped the gods would send them dreams revealing how they could be made well again. But, as it is today, prevention was better than cure, and so people wore lucky charms or **amulets**. They were designed to keep their wearers safe and well, and prevent harmful forces from hurting them.

There were many forms of treatment given out by doctors. More than 800 different **prescriptions** are known, most of which were made from **minerals**, plants and parts of animals (flesh, fat and milk). Some prescriptions included ingredients such as dirt from under a patient's fingernails, mouse droppings and mud from the River Nile. They probably weren't very effective! Doctors performed internal surgery with metal knives and probes. They sewed cuts together and dressed wounds with **linen** bandages, soaked in oil or honey to prevent infections from spreading, just as today's **antiseptics** do. Broken arms and legs were mended with wooden splints, tightly bound with linen.

Merchants

In about 1100 BC, an Egyptian **scribe** wrote about his country's trade and traders. He said, 'Merchants sail upstream and downstream (along the Nile), eager to carry goods from one place to another and to supply whatever is needed anywhere.' Not only was the scribe commenting on Egypt's economy, he was pointing out the importance of the River Nile – the 'great highway'.

A merchant's travels

Egypt was one of the wealthiest countries in the ancient world. In a good year, more grain was produced than was needed at home, and merchants exported (sold abroad) it to countries overseas. Egypt had an extensive trading network. Merchants sailed throughout the Mediterranean, calling at ports along the coasts of North Africa, Italy, Greece, Crete, Cyprus and the Middle East. It took about five days to sail on the open sea from Egypt to Greece. Merchants also sailed on the Red Sea, which brought them into contact with people in East Africa and Arabia.

In a country where land travel was difficult and slow, Egypt's mighty River Nile was the main means of transport. When the river level was high, it took about fourteen days for a boat to sail the 885 kilometres (550 miles) downstream between the cities of Thebes and Memphis. It took longer when the river level was low. The same distance overland took about 45 days. Boats carried large cargoes, whereas to move the same amount of goods by land meant using huge numbers of donkeys travelling together as a train.

The land of Punt

Egyptian merchants went on trading expeditions to a land they called Punt, where they obtained exotic goods such as gold, ebony (a black wood), elephant ivory, giraffe tails for fly whisks and animals, including monkeys and baboons. Slaves also came from here, as did **pygmies**, who became temple dancers. Where exactly was Punt? There is much disagreement about the location of this mysterious land, reached by sailing down the Red Sea. It seems to have been somewhere in east Africa – perhaps in the region of modern Ethiopia, Eritrea or Somalia.

As well as grain, merchants sold paper and rope made from **papyrus**, **linen** cloth and dried or pickled fish. They brought back materials that were needed in Egypt – copper, oil, timber, resin, perfumes and wine.

An economy based on barter

For most of ancient Egypt's history, merchants relied on an elaborate system of **barter**, where the price of goods was linked to their value in grain. Barter was based on a unit of measurement called the *deben*. A *deben* was a piece of copper weighing around 91 grams. During the period of Egyptian history known as the New Kingdom (about 1539 BC to 1075 BC), sacks of grain containing 34 kilograms were valued at 37 *deben* each. Once this value had been fixed, goods were said to be worth so many *deben*. A lowly pig was valued at 7 *deben*, while a cow cost 140 *deben* – 20 times as much.

When it came to buying and selling, people exchanged goods according to their *deben* value. So, for example, a merchant selling one pig knew he could swap it for goods to the value of 7 *deben*. He could have exchanged it for one plain shirt (5 *deben*), four chickens (1 *deben*) and one small **amulet** (1 *deben*). This system worked well inside Egypt, but not overseas, where the *deben* was not used. Here, some Egyptian merchants traded with foreign merchants using 'silent barter'. Each side laid down either more or fewer goods, until both parties felt they had reached the correct value for the goods on offer.

Dancers

Both men and women worked as professional dancers in ancient Egypt. The Egyptians thought dancing was a natural expression of joy. For example, when the harvest was gathered, farmers danced to give thanks to the gods, at parties dancers entertained the guests and people danced for pleasure in towns and villages. Dancing also played a part in the religious life of the Egyptians, and special dances were performed at ceremonies. The dancers were organized into troupes that worked for individual temples, or in the houses of the royal family and other powerful families.

The work of a female dancer

Dancing was one of the few professions open to women in ancient Egypt. Nothing is known about how women were trained to become dancers. However, there are many pictures that show girls dancing, and because of this it is thought that dancers began their training while they were children. In Egyptian society a girl was considered a child until around the age of twelve, when she married and became an adult.

It is from scenes like this tomb painting that we can find out more about ancient Egyptian dancers and musicians.

Female dancers performed in pairs and also in groups, but rarely on their own. By studying pictures of dancers, some of their dance steps and movements can be understood. They did cartwheels, handstands and back-bends, which to us seem more like acrobatics than dances. They ran and jumped, spun round and round, and waved their arms and wiggled their hips while standing still. In some dances they walked on their toes, with their arms curved above their heads, in others they threw balls to each other, or performed with mirrors and tambourines. Clearly, the dance routines that women performed were lively and energetic. Doubtless they learned their steps off by heart, just as dancers do today. As they danced, other women clapped their hands to keep the dancers in time, and musicians made music.

Music and song

Music was a part of daily life. It was used for worship, by labourers as they went about their work, and at parties and festivals. Musicians were mostly, but not always, women. They blew on pipes, plucked the strings of harps and lutes, banged on drums, shook rattles and tambourines, and struck bells and cymbals. Although the ancient tunes are now lost, Egyptian music may have sounded like modern Middle Eastern music – fast and high-pitched.

The work of a male dancer

Even less is known about men who worked as dancers. Again, from looking at pictures the Egyptians made, it's clear that men and women did not dance together. Some dances were performed only by men, such as a dance performed by a group of men called *muu* dancers. They were called upon by priests to dance at funerals, and appeared dressed in **kilts** and tall headdresses that may have been made from **papyrus** reeds. In their dance they made many high steps, as if stepping from one place to another. Perhaps their dance was meant to act as a guide to the spirit of the dead person, helping it to 'step' safely from this life and into the next.

The farmer

The most numerous workers in ancient Egypt were the country's thousands of farmers. They were among the illiterate masses, unable to read or write. They lived in simple houses made from **mud-brick**, and they owned few possessions. Despite their humble standard of living and their lowly place in society, way below that of **scribes** and doctors, they were probably ancient Egypt's most important workers. It was the country's farmers who produced food to feed the population – and everyone, from a slave to a pharaoh, had to eat. In ancient Egypt, farmers were respected and valued members of society.

The farming year

More than anything else, farmers needed fertile land to grow their crops, and to provide somewhere for their farm animals to live. This was exactly what the River Nile gave to them each and every year. The farming year was divided into three seasons of four months: the flood season, growing season and harvesting season.

A new farming year began in mid-June, when the River Nile began to flood. In its floodwater was a fine **silt**, washed down from mountains far to the south. By October the river had returned to its normal size, leaving the silt spread over the land as a layer of soft, black mud. To the Egyptians, this gift from the Nile represented the rebirth of the land.

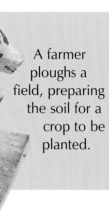

A farmer ploughs a field, preparing the soil for a crop to be planted.

Grain is tossed into the air in a process known as 'winnowing'. The unwanted husks are blown away by the wind.

Once the flood had gone down, the land was divided into small, square fields. These were allocated to farmers. Their main cereal crop was **emmer** (a kind of wheat), and barley was also grown. After ploughing the soil, seeds were scattered over the fields. Farm animals trampled the seeds into the soil, burying them out of sight of hungry birds.

Farmers harvested cereal crops in April and May, before the Nile flooded again in June. They cut the cereal ears off with the sharp flint blades of **sickles**, put them into baskets and took them to their farms. There, donkeys or oxen walked over the ears to separate the grain. The **nomes** and the government organized farming. Scribes kept records of how much grain was produced. A proportion of the harvest was paid in taxes to the pharaoh.

Animals on the farm

Farmers were also responsible for raising livestock. The most important farm animal was the cow, which grazed on pastures in marshy parts of the country. Not only was it a source of meat and milk, but it was also the main animal used for work on the farm. Farmers usually herded their cattle into pens at night, to protect them from wild beasts and thieves. Sheep and goats provided wool and hides, and pigs were kept for their meat. Some farmers raised poultry, such as geese, ducks, pigeons, quails and chickens. They gave meat and eggs, and also feathers that were used to adorn clothing.

Fishermen

The River Nile teemed with many kinds of fish, such as perch, catfish, eels and mullet. While some ancient Egyptians thought fish were **sacred** and could not be eaten, others relied on them for a large part of their diet. Fish was eaten both fresh and dried, but first it had to be caught.

A fisherman on the Nile

Fishing had been a part of daily life since before the time of the pharaohs, but it became particularly important during the period of Egyptian history known as the Middle Kingdom (about 1938 BC to 1600 BC). Fishermen were very low members of society, and many people looked down on them. The fish they caught were mostly eaten by ordinary people who could not afford meat.

Sometimes a net was stretched between two boats, and the fishermen worked together to bring in the catch. Net fishing was good for catching small fish.

Danger in the water

Crocodiles lived in the River Nile, and were a danger to an unwary fisherman who might fall, or be pushed, into the water. It wasn't only fishermen who had to be careful, since these dreaded animals were just as likely to attack a person collecting water, or even a farmer tending to his crops on the land. At least one **mummy** of a girl has been found with missing legs. Scientists who examined the body have wondered if the unfortunate girl might have been the victim of a crocodile attack.

Fishermen had several ways of trapping a catch. They sailed on the River Nile in rafts or canoes made from **papyrus** reeds, and fished with small nets attached to wooden frames that they scooped into the water. They used large drag-nets, too, which were taken out by boat and hauled in by men on the shore.

Large fish were caught with spears and harpoons that were stabbed at them as they swam close to the boats. In some parts of the river, bottle-shaped baskets made from willow branches were weighed down with stones and sunk into the water. When fish swam into them they became trapped. A more leisurely method of fishing was with rods and lines strung with lots of hooks, where fishermen waited for fish to take the bait.

There was one fish that Egyptian fishermen dreaded catching – a species of catfish armed with a poisonous spine on one of its fins. Even crocodiles were said to be afraid of it. There was time for some fun, too. To relieve the hours of waiting, fishermen pushed their rivals into the water!

After the fish had been caught, they were clubbed to death. Fishermen might take their catch straight to market, still fresh. Or they might gut them, flatten them and hang them in the sun to dry, or salt them and pickle them in oil. Egypt's merchants sold great quantities of dried and pickled fish to other countries.

The hunter

The ancient Egyptians hunted their land's wildlife both for food and for sport, but it was not always that way. Long before farming and village life had spread to Egypt – the time before Egypt had pharaohs and pyramids – bands of **nomadic hunter-gatherers** roamed the Nile Valley, hunting wild cattle, hartebeest (a sort of antelope), deer and hares. In the desert they caught gazelles, antelopes and even jackals and desert cats. They hunted for their own survival. Slowly, however, a new way of life emerged in Egypt. People settled down in villages. They grew crops on the land, and tamed wild animals to use on their farms. They no longer needed to hunt in order to survive.

Nebamun was a nobleman who died in about 1400 BC. This picture was painted on the walls of his tomb. It shows him hunting for birds in the marshes of the River Nile. His wife and daughter are with him, as is his cat. Nebamun is using a wooden throwing-stick shaped like a snake to kill birds, which his cat is catching as they fall from the sky. Although Nebamun was probably hunting for sport, this picture shows us the equipment a hunter would have used.

Hunting for hippopotamuses

The shallow, marshy waters along the edge of the River Nile were home to the hippopotamus. The female hippo was associated with Taweret, the goddess of women and childbirth. Despite being a **sacred** animal, it was regarded as a nuisance by farmers, since it ate and trampled their crops. For this reason, male and female hippos were hunted. Hunters used special harpoons to kill a hippo. When their harpoon struck, the harpoon head snapped off inside the animal's body. Attached to the harpoon head were ropes. Men on the riverbank pulled on the ropes, dragging the hippo ashore, where it was clubbed to death.

Hunting for food

Hunting for smaller prey was the work of ordinary working people. They caught a wide variety of birds in the marshes along the River Nile, such as wild ducks, geese, herons, pelicans and cranes. For these people, hunting was a means of providing food. They hunted from boats, and used cats to scare the birds so the hunters knew where they were. Birds were killed with arrows and **throwing-sticks**. They were collected from the water by the hunters' families. Flocks of small birds such as quail were caught in nets laid on the ground and baited with grain. Birds were attracted by the free food, and when the net was closed they were trapped.

Hunting for sport

Hunting for big game (lions, wild bulls, rhinoceroses, gazelles, antelopes, ostriches and even elephants) became a favourite activity for pharaohs and nobles. It was a sport carried out for pleasure by only the wealthiest members of Egyptian society.

The baker

Everyone in ancient Egypt ate bread. It was the staple (main) food of rich and poor alike. Until about 2000 BC bread was baked by women for their families at home, or by servants who worked for the nobles and the pharaoh. However, as the demand for bread increased, bakeries were built to make bread for towns, villages and temples, and people began to work full-time as bakers.

From grain to flour

Most bread was made from **emmer**-wheat, the main cereal crop grown by Egypt's farmers. Grain was brought to the bakeries from **granaries**, where it was stored. Making bread was busy teamwork. Everyone who worked at a bakery had their own job to do.

First, men crushed the grain by pounding it with wooden poles. This was to break the grain down into smaller pieces, removing the bran (coarse husks). Then, the crushed grain was ground into flour. Women did this by rubbing the grain between grindstones. As the stones moved, the grain turned into a white powder – flour. It was not the sort of fine flour we know today. The flour of the ancient Egyptians was coarse. This was not just because it was badly

From models like this we can learn a great deal about the work of Egyptian bakers. Both men and women worked in the country's bakeries. The bread and cakes they baked were eaten on the day they were made. Fresh supplies were baked all the time, to make sure no one went short of food.

ground, but because it contained microscopic pieces of stone which had broken away from the grindstones, and also sand particles blown in by the wind. Even though flour was sieved, 'foreign bodies' still ended up in the bread and mouths of the Egyptians. We know this because ancient bread has been examined, and also because the worn and scratched teeth of the Egyptians show tell-tale signs that they chewed gritty food.

From flour to bread

To make bread dough, the baker mixed flour with water and a little salt. It was then ready to shape by hand into loaves and bake on stones placed over a fire, or inside tall ovens made from clay. This was a quick and easy way to make unleavened bread (bread that does not rise). It produced flat pancake-shaped loaves like modern pitta bread. If the baker wanted his bread to rise, he added yeast to the dough, and left it to stand for a while before shaping it. Yeast came from breweries and in ancient Egypt bakeries and breweries were often built close to each other.

Beer and beer-making

Egyptian beer was a slightly alcoholic drink, and everyone drank it, including children. It was a nutritious food that was thick and soupy, and an important part of the Egyptians' diet. Women brewed beer from barley grain, or stale barley-bread, water and yeast. Like bread, it was flavoured with honey, spices or herbs. It took a few days for the mixture to mature, during which time it was strained through a cloth to remove any bits. Beer did not keep long, and was drunk soon after it had been made.

Loaves made by the ancient Egyptians, like these, have been found in their tombs, where they were placed as offerings to feed the dead as they travelled into the afterlife. Bakers produced 40 to 50 different types of loaves and cakes. Some were made with hollows in the top to hold a serving of beans or vegetables. Others were shaped like triangles, and some were wafer-thin. They could all be flavoured by adding honey, sesame seeds, dates, eggs and herbs to the dough.

Carpenters and coffin-makers

Trees such as acacias, tamarisks, palms, figs and sycamores all grew well in Egypt. However, there were not enough of them to provide craftspeople, especially carpenters and coffin-makers, with all the timber they needed. The tree valued more than any other for its timber was the cedar – and it did not grow in Egypt. Merchants travelled north to the Lebanon to trade for supplies of cedar timber, which was in great demand by Egypt's woodworkers. Other types of timber from foreign lands brought into Egypt included ebony, pine and juniper. All had their uses.

Inside a carpenter's workshop

A carpenter's workshop was a busy place, with men doing many different jobs. This is how they worked on one tree-trunk. First, they lopped branches off the trunk using a bronze axe. Then they sawed the trunk into planks. To do this, the trunk was lifted into an upright position and tied to a post set into the ground. The post held the tree-trunk steady while the carpenter and his assistant sawed it from top to bottom using a bronze saw. Each tree-trunk produced several rough planks. Next, the planks were smoothed with a bronze tool called an adze. It chipped away at the surface until it was smooth and even all over. The timber was then ready.

A **relief** of carpenters at work on a ship. They are smoothing the sides of the vessel with their tools.

A coffin-maker's work

Some carpenters specialized in making timber coffins, which were containers for **mummified** bodies of dead people. The most expensive coffins were made from highly prized cedar wood. Several types of timber coffins were made. The first and simplest were made from planks joined together to make rectangular boxes with lids. Later, coffins in the shape of a body were made. Wealthy people sometimes had 'nests' of coffins, with several body-shaped coffins fitting one inside the other. Carpenters who made these were highly skilled workers. Most coffins were painted on the outside and the inside, with both words and pictures.

Wood for furniture

Wood was expensive because it was in short supply. It was mostly used to make pieces of furniture, statues and small objects, and was rarely used to make buildings. However, some wealthy people did have timber columns in their homes to hold up their ceilings.

All kinds of furniture were made from wood, especially beds, chests, chairs and stools. Pieces of wood were joined together with wooden dowels (pegs) and joints that slotted into each other. Furniture made for wealthy people was often decorated with carved or painted designs. Poorer people, if they had any furniture at all, had simple, undecorated pieces. Carpenters could make a cheap wood look like a more expensive wood by colouring its surface. They also invented veneering, where a thin slice of expensive wood was glued onto cheaper wood. Veneering was an economical way of using wood – in the hands of a skilled carpenter, a little bit could be made to go a long way. Because wood was costly, carpenters made sure nothing went to waste.

A painted wooden coffin in the shape of a person. This mummy belonged to Takhebkhenem and is decorated with colourful pictures of gods and **hieroglyphs**.

Spinners and weavers

People wore clothes made mostly from **linen** cloth. Sheep's wool was used to make some items of clothing, though it was never as popular as linen. Cotton did not come into use until the very end of the ancient Egyptians' long history. Both men and women made clothes. They spun and weaved plant fibres to make cloth, and shaped the cloth into clothes, and into sheets and bandages which were used to wrap **mummies**.

Picking and spinning flax

The flax plant, from which linen was made, was picked in the winter months by groups of men and women who harvested it together. It was grown as a crop. The plants, which were about a metre tall, were pulled up whole, roots and all. The best time to go flax-pulling was when the blue flowers of the plants were open – young plants such as these produced the best fibres for spinning.

The uprooted plants were collected into bundles and taken to a weaving workshop. Workers pulled the bundles through large wooden combs that stripped the tops from the plants, and shredded the stems into fibres. The bundles were combed several times to produce bunches of fibres. This was hard work, carried out by men and women. Children gathered up the seeds that fell from the flowers. Some seeds were saved for planting the next year's crop; others were crushed for their linseed oil that was used in medicine.

Women work weaving cloth on horizontal looms and others spin thread. This model was found in the tomb of Meketre in Deir El-Bahri.

Groups of women worked together to turn the fibres into yarn (thread) for weaving. Some women sat on the floor of the weaving workshop, with piles of flax fibres in front of them. They took handfuls of fibres and rolled them against their thighs. This action twisted the fibres into balls. Other women, who worked as spinners, teased a few fibres from the balls, pulling them out with their fingers and twisting them together to make a single thread. The spinners wound the thread onto wooden spindles, and it was then ready for weaving.

Clothing

Because Egypt had (and still has) a warm, dry climate, there was no need for the ancient Egyptians to wear lots of clothes. The ancient Greeks called them 'the sun-baked race' simply because they did not cover their bodies with much clothing. Men went about their daily work dressed only in a loincloth (cloth worn round the hips) or a short **kilt**, leaving their chests, arms and legs exposed to the sun. Women wore tunics, young children did too, or went about naked. Most clothes were white, but some were dyed with plant and **mineral** extracts to make them red, blue, and yellow.

Weaving the cloth

The spun flax was woven on looms to make linen cloth. The first looms used by the ancient Egyptians were horizontal looms pegged out on the floor of the weaving workshop. At this time, women weavers worked at them by crouching on the floor. Later, upright looms came into use. Weaving on these much bigger looms became men's work.

Workers who operated upright looms sat at benches, producing cloth that was about 170 centimetres wide. Several grades of linen were made by weavers, ranging from coarse cloth for ordinary folk to fine, high-quality cloth used for the clothes of the nobles and the pharaoh. It was said that a sheet of the finest linen was so smooth that it could be pulled through a finger ring without getting stuck.

The jeweller

Jewellery was made by men in workshops. It is one of ancient Egypt's best-known crafts because the materials from which it was made, such as gold and precious stones, have survived to the present day. The range of objects made by Egypt's jewellers was quite amazing – from tiny beads and **amulets** to large ceremonial pieces for the pharaoh and his family. Both men and women wore jewellery. Some items were believed to have magical properties and were worn to protect the wearer from harm, while others were worn for their beauty.

Bead-making in a jeweller's workshop

Several types of **semi-precious stones** were used by jewellers, including green feldspar, red jasper, orange-red carnelian, mauve amethyst and dark blue lapis lazuli (see box). To make beads, chunks of rock were hit with stone hammers to break them into

Jewellers at work. Note how some men are pulling bows backwards and forwards, twisting drills into the beads on their workbenches. As the drills turned round and round, jewellers sprinkled grains of quartz into the little holes that started to form in the beads. The rough quartz wore away at the bead, until it had made a hole all the way through it. Jewellers were sometimes shown as dwarves in art, but whether there were dwarf-jewellers in reality is still a puzzle.

Lapis lazuli – a precious blue stone

There was a stone used in making jewellery that was as highly prized as gold. The ancient Egyptians called it *khesbed*, and we know it as lapis lazuli. It was dark blue in colour and came from mines in modern Afghanistan, some 3200 kilometres (2000 miles) to the east. It reached Egypt by coming overland along trade routes, changing hands several times before being bought by Egyptian merchants who sold it to the country's jewellers. Such was the rarity and value of lapis that the Egyptians tried to copy it by making a lookalike substance from crushed quartz. This was **faience**, a blue or green material used for inexpensive items. It could be shaped and fired like pottery.

smaller pieces. The pieces were a little bigger than the beads they were to become. A jeweller selected the pieces he wanted, and fixed them into a layer of plaster on his workbench. The plaster held the beads firmly in place. Then, using a **bow drill** he began to drill into the beads, making a hole right through them. Afterwards, **quartz** powder was used to polish the beads until they were smooth all over. They were then ready for stringing to make colourful necklaces and collars.

Making beads was a long and probably boring job. We get an idea of this from what a father wrote to his son, Khety. He said, 'The jeweller has to drill all kinds of hard stones. By the time he has finished he is tired and weak. He has to sit with his legs folded and back bent all day.'

Gold – the metal of the gods

Gold was the most valued metal used in jewellery making. Because it did not go dull it was thought to be a divine metal, a metal of the gods. Gold **ore**, from Egypt's mines, was heated in furnaces. The temperature needed to reach more than 1000° Celsius before liquid gold ran from the ore and into moulds. Once the jewellers had extracted the gold, it was ready for use. It was beaten into gold leaf (wafer-thin sheets of gold) which was applied over wooden statues, coffins and items of furniture, making them appear to be made of solid gold. Or it could be cast into objects such as rings, amulets and masks worn by **mummies**.

Who built the tombs of ancient Egypt?

The great stone buildings of ancient Egypt, such as temples and pyramids, are still there for us to see today. Less important buildings, such as the **mud-brick** houses lived in by the ordinary people, have long since disappeared. They were worn away to dust by wind and water. Egypt's stone buildings are splendid examples of the **masons'** work, unaltered after thousands of years. Before the stonemasons could create these long-lasting structures, the rock from which they were made had to be **quarried** from the ground. This bone-breaking, dangerous work was carried out by quarrymen.

Working in Egypt's stone quarries

There were plentiful supplies of building stone in Egypt, especially limestone and sandstone. Only the best stone was used, and to reach it workers would tunnel into mountains or scrape away the surface layers to reveal it on the ground. Once they had reached the layer of stone they wanted, they set about quarrying it.

This is a view of the Khafra quarry at Giza. Huge blocks of stone were quarried here for use in pyramid statue building.

Building with mud

The traditional building material used by the ancient Egyptians was mud-brick. It was used for houses, and also for tombs and even pyramids. Mud-brick was made from clay mixed with water and chopped straw. Brickmakers then pressed the clay mixture into brick-shaped wooden frames. Then they pressed the bricks out, and placed them in long rows to bake hard in the sun. Mud-bricks came in several sizes, a little smaller than bricks we use today. They were light and easy to build with. Builders stuck them together with clay mixed with sand.

For most of ancient Egypt's long history, quarrymen worked with chisels made from copper or bronze. Only towards the end of their history did they use iron chisels. They hammered at their chisels with wooden mallets or with stones. Another vital tool was the stone pick, or hammerstone. It was a lump of hard stone (usually basalt or dolerite) which was held in the hand or tied to a wooden handle. Picks started off as sharp tools, but with use they became round and blunt, and were thrown away.

To quarry a block of stone, quarrymen used their chisels and stone picks to score a wide, deep slot all around it. Then they cut smaller slots around its base. Wooden levers were forced into the slots, and by pulling on them the block broke away from its parent rock.

Quarry workshops

Cutting stone blocks was the start of a long, slow process of preparing them for use. Some blocks were destined for building sites; others were to become statues. Either way, when they came out of the quarry they were rough, and so the next thing that happened was to smooth them. Stonemasons pecked away at their surfaces with hammerstones and polished them with powdered **quartz**. When this was over, the block or statue was ready to be transported to where it was needed. Sometimes the masons never got this far. There are many examples of half-finished statues and **obelisks** lying abandoned in quarries. They broke while they were being worked on, and could not be mended: it was time to start all over again.

Pyramid builders

The pyramids of Egypt were massive tombs built for the pharaohs of Egypt's Old Kingdom. The 'golden age' of pyramid building lasted for around 800 years, starting around 2600 BC. During this time some 90 pyramids were built, made from both stone and **mud-brick**. The most famous pyramids are a group of three at Giza. The biggest of the group, and the largest pyramid ever made, is the Great Pyramid. It was the tomb of the pharaoh Khufu, and was built by a highly organized workforce.

The Great Pyramid workforce

Modern calculations have shown that it took no more than 25,000 men to build the Great Pyramid, not the 100,000 claimed by the ancient historian Herodotus (see page 6). About 5000 skilled men worked full-time on the project, such as **masons** and other craftsmen. The rest of the workforce was part-time. These were the manual labourers who came from other jobs to work on what was a national building project. They stayed for about three months at a time, before returning home to their normal lives, and others took their place.

The Great Pyramid at Giza is one of the seven wonders of the world. It is on the outskirts of Cairo, Egypt's modern capital. It is constructed from over 2,300,000 blocks of stone, each one weighing an average of 2.5 tonnes. It took around twenty years to build this pyramid, with one block of stone being raised into place every two to three minutes during a ten-hour working day.

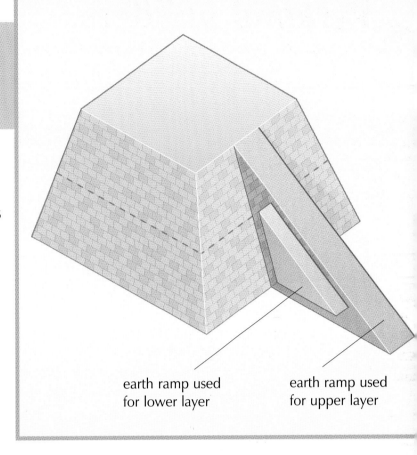

Pyramids may have been built using sloping ramps of earth to get blocks of stone to the top.

earth ramp used for lower layer

earth ramp used for upper layer

Stone haulers, stone setters and stonemasons

Blocks of stone, each weighing about 2.5 tonnes (about the weight of 40 adults) were moved from the quarry to the Great Pyramid building site on wooden sledges. Teams of stone haulers pulled the sledges. It has been calculated that a team of twenty stone haulers took an hour to drag a block of stone from the **quarry**, and then return with the empty sledge. When the blocks were at the site, they were dragged up one or more sloping ramps of earth built against the sides of the pyramid. Once at the top of a ramp, **stone setters** took over and moved the blocks into place. It took about ten setters to handle each block. Finally, stonemasons trimmed the blocks, cutting pieces off them to make sure they were a good fit.

Painful work

Skeletons of the manual workers who built the Great Pyramid have been found, and they show that the men suffered accidents and injury, such as broken limbs. The fractures had healed well. At least one man had lost an arm, and he had survived. All of this is evidence of the skill of Egypt's doctors 4500 years ago, who were able to treat serious injuries. Many of the skeletons show signs of back trouble – their spines are curved, possibly caused by years of pushing and pulling heavy blocks of stone. These men would have walked slightly bent over.

Egyptian artists

◄► ◄► ◄► ◄► ◄► ◄► ◄► ◄► ◄► ◄► ◄► ◄► ◄► ◄► ◄► ◄► ◄► ◄► ◄►

The ancient Egyptians excelled in producing works of art. Painters decorated tomb walls, coffins and statues made of wood or stone. Sculptors worked in stone, carving lifelike figures of people, gods and animals. They made statues, and also carved **reliefs** on the walls of temples. Painting and sculpture was teamwork, where people worked together, each man doing a specific job.

How a sculptor carved a stone statue

A sculptor's workshop was a noisy, dusty place. A block of stone for a statue came from the **quarry**. Sometimes a block might have been roughly shaped into a statue at the quarry. Other times it arrived unshaped. At the workshop men using hammerstones pecked away at the block, chipping off small pieces. It took several days before their work was finished and the statue was 'roughed out'. Then, they used copper or bronze chisels to carve fine details, such as eyes, ears and fingers. They had to be careful not to hit their chisels too hard, or in the wrong place, otherwise they might do serious damage. Finally, the statue was smoothed all over. Sculptors used polishing stones to rub **quartz** grains over its surface until all traces of roughness had gone. The statue was then passed to painters for colouring.

Artists painted the human figure as if it could be seen from several different angles. The head, face and limbs were shown from the side. The eyes, shoulders and chest were shown from the front, and the hips, legs and feet from the side. Artists painted this way to make the body seem as lifelike as possible.

Making art by squares

To make a painting or a statue of a standing person, the first thing an artist did was draw a grid of squares on the wall, or block of stone he was going to use. Grids contained 18 or 21 squares and each square measured one palm wide by one palm high (a palm was the distance across four fingers and the thumb of the figure being represented). Grids helped artists to work out the correct proportions for the human figure, with body parts falling on, or between, specific squares.

How a tomb painter worked

Before a tomb painter began his work, a draughtsman sketched the picture onto the wall, using a grid of squares to guide him (see box). He often practised the drawing on pieces of pottery before starting the real picture. A draughtsman was a 'writer of outlines' who drew the picture in a bold line. First, he drew the outline in red. Then, when he was happy with the picture, he drew the final outline in black. He was careful to follow the rules of drawing, such as making the picture of the tomb owner bigger than pictures of less important people.

A painter coloured the outline in. He painted with brushes made from the stems of reeds. He chewed their ends to fray them, so they would hold paint. Colours had meanings. White stood for joy; yellow was for gold and the gods; pale yellow was for women's skin; brownish-red was for men's skin; red was for blood and life, and also for evil and chaos; green was for water and new life; blue was the sky; and black was for the soil and fertility. Colours were made from plants and **minerals**, and were mixed with water and egg (the egg helped the colours stick to the wall).

The place of artists in society

Most artists (sculptors, draughtsmen and painters) worked directly for the pharaoh. They could be 'lent' out by him to work for temples and private individuals. Their work was highly valued. They received gifts of land, cattle and valuables, making them wealthy and privileged members of society.

The embalmer

The ancient Egyptians believed in life after death. They thought that a person who had died would be reborn, and would live forever in the afterlife. For that to succeed, they believed a person's body had to be preserved, so that it could act as a 'home' for the body's spirits to return to. It was for this reason that the Egyptians perfected the craft of making **mummies**.

Mummy-makers at work

Mummies were made for about 3000 years. The first were made around 2600 BC and the last around AD 400. It was during the 500 years of the New Kingdom (about 1539 BC to 1075 BC) that Egypt's **embalmers** produced the best mummies of all. It took them about 70 days to make a mummy.

Embalmers worked in tents in the open air, close to the River Nile, from where they took water to wash and clean bodies. A dead person was placed on a flat wood or stone table. Then embalmers removed the person's brain with long bronze hooks. The brain was pulled out through the person's nose, and from the hole at the base of the skull where it joins the spine. A mixture of **resin**, bee's wax and sweet-smelling oils was then poured into the empty skull. As it cooled, it set hard.

Thin linen strips were used to wrap a mummified body. They were often torn from worn out clothes and furnishings. The more important the person, the more care was taken over the bandaging. The body was wrapped in layer after layer, covering it from head to toe.

Mourning the dead

If the family of a dead person could afford to, they might hire professional mourners to come and stay with them while the body was being embalmed and bandaged. Women worked as full-time mourners. It was their job to grieve openly both inside and outside the dead person's house, and then to go with the body to the tomb. Mourners threw dust on their heads, waved their arms, tugged at their clothes, scratched their cheeks, cried and wailed out loud.

Next, embalmers made a deep cut on the left side of the tummy and took out the lungs, liver, stomach and intestines. The heart was left inside the body, because it was thought to be the centre of a person's intelligence and emotions. The empty body was then washed out, and filled and covered with **natron**. Natron absorbed water and other body liquids.

The body was left to dry out for 40 days, after which it was made to look lifelike again. The abdomen and chest were packed with **linen**, sawdust, wood shavings and even mud, to give the body a 'natural' shape. The skin was rubbed with oils to make it soft and supple. The nostrils, ears and mouth were plugged with linen. The eyes were pressed down into the head, balls of linen were pushed into the eye sockets and the eyelids were closed. The cut in the abdomen was sealed with a layer of wax, or covered with a thin sheet of gold. Once all this had been done, the body was wrapped in linen bandages, placed in a coffin and taken for burial in a tomb.

A person's vital organs were packed into four individual containers, known as **canopic jars**. The jars were in the shape of the sons of the god Horus. It was their job to protect the organs. The intestines were looked after by the falcon-headed Qebehsenuef. The jackal-headed Duamutef protected the stomach. The lungs were cared for by the ape-headed Hapy. The human-headed Imsety looked after the person's liver.

41

How do we know?

It is people who make history, not buildings or objects. The **mummies** of ancient Egypt are the men, women and children who made Egypt's civilization great. They are the real treasures of the past. Advances in science and technology are making it possible to find out more about ancient people, and to understand their private lives. Egyptian mummies now 'speak' to us, telling us wonderful things about their lives and work.

A woman called Asru

At Manchester Museum, England, there is a mummy of a woman named Asru, who died around 700 BC. The writing on her coffin said she had worked as a singer in a temple. Her dried-out body has been scientifically studied. Probes have entered her chest, abdomen and skull, and tiny amounts of tissue have been removed for examination. Miniature cameras have roamed around inside her body, photographing details that would otherwise be impossible to see. X-ray pictures have revealed her skeleton and teeth, and a **CAT-scan** has given three-dimensional pictures of her entire body, inside and out. From these images a plastic copy of Asru's skull has been made, shaped in every detail by a cutting laser beam, and her face has been reconstructed. The police have even taken her finger- and toe-prints.

Techniques like this help us to build a picture of the working people of ancient Egypt. We will never have a complete picture, and

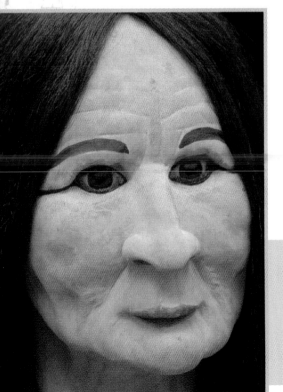

A medical artist rebuilt Asru's face over a model skull. The face, made from clay, shows a woman in her sixties. Her cheeks are sunken because of her bad teeth. She had an over-bite, where her top teeth came over her bottom teeth. The artist has shown this by the way in which Asru's lips have been reconstructed.

The life of Asru

From the evidence they collected, scientists have worked out what sort of life Asru lived, almost 3000 years ago. They knew she had worked as a singer, and the evidence agreed with this. Her fingerprints were not worn or damaged, so it was clear she had not done heavy manual work. Her toe-prints were also in good condition, so it seems she had not done much barefoot dancing as part of her temple duties. X-rays revealed she had arthritis in her fingers and knees, and that she had hurt her back – painful problems for Asru, especially as she grew older.

Her teeth were in poor condition. Some had fallen out, some had holes in them and most were badly worn after a lifetime of eating gritty bread. She probably had terrible toothache. She would also have been short of breath, since she had a lung disease caused by breathing in tiny particles of sand. It probably meant she also had a bad cough. Asru also had three different kinds of parasitic worms in her intestines, lungs and bladder. The tapeworm in her lungs may have entered her body through eating undercooked pork meat. The worms would have caused Asru to lose blood, leaving her tired and weak.

Despite her health problems, Asru lived to an old age. She was in her sixties when she died. Many women in Egypt did not live much beyond their late twenties – some died giving birth to children. Perhaps it was because of her work as a singer that she lived so long. This kind of job, practised in the comfortable surroundings of a temple would have been the work of a woman from a well-to-do family.

archaeologists are making new discoveries all the time. We can, however, unearth evidence of the variety of different jobs in ancient Egypt. We can find out more about the hard lives and the achievements of the people who did those jobs.

Asru's mummy has been at Manchester Museum since 1825. When it came to England it had already been unwrapped, and the bandages had been thrown away. As part of Asru's **embalming** process, sweet-smelling **resins** were wrapped between her bandages. Today, almost 3000 years after her death, her body still smells of them, possibly myrrh and frankincense.

Timeline

◄► ◄► ◄► ◄► ◄► ◄► ◄► ◄► ◄► ◄► ◄► ◄► ◄► ◄► ◄► ◄► ◄►

All dates are BC. Pharaoh's dates refer to reigns.
All dates are approximate as they vary from source to source.

Before 5000
Early settlers farmed and built towns along the Nile.

About 3000
Lower and Upper Egypt united. **Dynasties** (ruling families) 1,2 and 3.

2575 to 2130 The Old Kingdom
Pyramids are built at Giza. Dynasties 4 to 8.
Trading expeditions, war with Libyans.

2130 to 1938 First Intermediate Period
A time of weak rulers. Dynasties 9, 10 and 11.

1938 to 1600 Middle Kingdom
Power of pharaohs is restored. Dynasties 12 and 13.

1630 to 1540 Second Intermediate Period
Dynasties 14 to 17.

1539 to 1075 New Kingdom
Dynasties 18 to 20. Egypt's power at its height.
One of the rulers at this time was Hatshepsut (died about 1458), who
sends a famous expedition to the land of Punt.
Reign of Akhenaten (Amenhotep IV) in the 1300s is a time of religious
upheaval, as his new sun-god replaces old gods of Egypt.
Tutankhamen rules from 1333 to 1323.
Ramses II (1279 to 1213) known as Ramses the Great.

1075 to 665 Third Intermediate Period
Dynasties 21 to 25. Pharaohs of Libyan heritage rule Egypt (dynasties 21
to 23). Dynasty 25 were Kushite rulers.

664 to 332 Late period, a time of foreign rule
Dynasties 26 to 30.
Local rulers struggle for power. Dynasty 27 consisted of Persian kings who
did not live in Egypt, but styled themselves as pharaohs.
Dynasties 28 to 30 were native rulers.
332 Alexander the Great from Greece conquers the country.
305, a new dynasty is founded, under Ptolemy, a Greek.
51 Cleopatra becomes joint ruler of Egypt with her brother. She rules
alone from 47.
31 Defeat by Roman fleet at sea battle of Actium ends Egypt's power.
Romans make Egypt a Roman province.

Sources and further reading

Sources

British Museum Dictionary of Ancient Egypt, Ian Shaw and Paul Nicholson
(British Museum, 1995)

Life of the Ancient Egyptians, Eugen Strouhal
(Liverpool University Press, 1997)

People of the Pharaohs: from Peasant to Courtier, Hilary Wilson
(Michael O'Mara, 1997)

The Private Lives of the Pharaohs, Joyce Tyldesley
(Channel 4 Books, 2000)

Further reading

Ancient Egypt: Family Life, Stewart Ross
(Hodder Wayland, 2001)

Encyclopedia of Ancient Egypt, Gill Harvey and Struan Reid
(Usborne, 2001)

Eyewitness Guides: Ancient Egypt, George Hart
(Dorling Kindersley, 1990)

Megabites: Mummies and the Secrets of Ancient Egypt, John Malam
(Dorling Kindersley, 2001)

Glossary

◀▶ ◀▶ ◀▶ ◀▶ ◀▶ ◀▶ ◀▶ ◀▶ ◀▶ ◀▶ ◀▶ ◀▶ ◀▶ ◀▶ ◀▶ ◀▶ ◀▶ ◀

amulet good luck charm used to protect the wearer from harm

antiseptics substance that prevents the growth of disease-causing bacteria

archaeologist person who finds out about the past by looking for the remains of buildings and other objects, often beneath the ground

barter trading system in which goods are exchanged for each other and not money

bow drill type of drill shaped like an archer's bow, operated by hand

canopic jars four jars that held the mummified stomach, liver, lungs and intestines of a dead person

CAT-scan computerized axial tomography (CAT), a method of examining a body that uses X-rays to make detailed pictures of the internal organs

demotic style of handwriting which developed from the hieratic script and which could be written quickly

diagnosis identification of a disease

dynasty series of pharaohs from related families. Egypt's pharaohs formed 30 dynasties.

embalm process of preserving a dead body to prevent it from decaying

emmer wheat commonly grown in ancient Egypt

faience material formed from a paste of crushed quartz which had a glazed surface. It was fired hard in a kiln, and was used to make small objects such as amulets.

granary storage place for grain

hieratic script, used for everyday writing which was quick to write. It was derived from hieroglyphs.

hieroglyphs oldest writing script used in ancient Egypt, consisting of signs that refer to the meaning and sound of words

kilt short skirt-like garment

linen fabric made from the fibres of the flax plant

maladies illnesses

mason person who cuts, shapes and lays stones; a builder who works with stone

mineral solid natural substance that comes from the ground

mud-brick brick made from clay, often mixed with chopped straw or grass, and dried hard by the Sun. Used in dry climates for the construction of buildings.

mummy animal or human body preserved by drying

natron type of salt that occurred naturally in Egypt and which was used to dry bodies during the process of mummification

nomadic hunter-gatherers people who wander across the land hunting prey and gathering wild crops

nomarch government official who controlled one of Egypt's many local districts, or nomes

nome one of 42 local districts in Egypt, under the authority of a governor called a nomarch

obelisk tall stone with a pyramid-shaped top that was a symbol of the Sun's rays

ore substance which metal or precious minerals are taken from

overseer supervisor

papyrus water reed used to make a type of writing paper, baskets, ropes, sandals and medicine

pharaoh king or queen of ancient Egypt

prescription instructions about medicine needed for a patient written by a doctor

pygmies very small people

quarry to take stone out of the ground

quartz hard kind of mineral

relief picture cut into stone, so that figures stand out

resin sticky substance obtained from the sap of trees and plants

sacred something that is holy or connected with a god

scribe person trained to read and write

semi-precious stone hard stone used in jewellery-making such as carnelian, amethyst and lapis lazuli

sickle stone or metal knife, usually crescent shaped, used to cut crops

silt fine sediment carried in water which settles to form mud and soil

stone setter person who puts (sets) stones in place when a building is being constructed

symptoms signs of sickness

throwing-stick shaped and weighted stick thrown by hunters at their prey

vizier highest official in Egypt. He informed the pharaoh about everything that happened and saw that the king's instructions were carried out.

Index